A Mother's PRAYER

A Mother's PRAYER

Inspiring True Stories to Warm the Heart

Jean Holbrook Mathews, Margot Hovley,
Jodi Marie Robinson, Michele Ashman Bell, Sandra Grey,
Karen Tuft, Stephanie Dibb Sorensen,
Susan Easton Black, Josi S. Kilpack, Jeri Gilchrist,
Toni Sorenson

Covenant Communications, Inc.

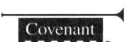

Contents

The Miracle of the Washing Machine
Jean Holbrook Mathews

MOTHERS ARE MIRACLE WORKERS. EVEN when they have much less than later generations, they learn to "make do."

When I and many of my friends were first married, we didn't have six credit cards, let alone one, and if someone did have one, they couldn't even pay the bill if they used it. We drove our cars until the air showed through the tires. We rinsed the weevil out of the rice or macaroni, cut down our dresses to make our oldest child a new shirt or dress for kindergarten, and cut off starts from our mothers' houseplants to start our own, which then promptly died. We often cut our own hair and washed our own cars and dogs. We gave gifts in boxes from stores that had closed five years earlier, and from Christmas to Christmas, we gave and received bows multiple times on those boxes. One of the biggest challenges came when we struggled to raise small children born close together *without disposable diapers.*

My mother taught me some useful tips, such as the fact that a plastic hair curler inserted in one of the flaps of the carburetor would improve the chances of getting the car to start on a cold morning. Though I sewed out of necessity so my children would be clothed when they went to school, my mother was a seamstress who made my skills pale by comparison. She made my graduation dress and my sister's wedding dress without patterns. Her quiet, practical wisdom was a special blessing when I became a young mother.

Recognizing Erma Bombeck's wisdom, who stated, "Children make life important," my husband and I knew we wanted a family despite our limited financial resources. Once we set our minds to creating a family, we were determined to acquire those children any way we could. That meant that after my many miscarriages, we decided to apply with the Salt Lake County Welfare Department to become foster parents. Within less than a month, we had twin boys placed on our couch and their limited belongings sitting in a little pile on the floor. The social worker wished us luck and then rushed out of the house as if he was afraid we might change our minds.

These two little boys couldn't walk yet, and one wouldn't eat. He wanted his bottle and only his bottle. They had never been introduced to semisolid food, and the worn-out cloth diapers that came with them were as thin as cheese cloth.

Before that first day had ended, I had begun to learn just how many diapers two little boys could go through in a day, especially when I had to fold at least two of them together to be absorbent enough to do the job.

These two souls had been with us only about forty-eight hours when my mother recognized that I was in bigger trouble than I dreamed. Our little apartment was in a four-plex and didn't have laundry facilities. We were a one-car family, and the nearest Laundromat was a mile or two away. So before the diaper pail overflowed to the point that we were pushed completely out of the bathroom, she came to my rescue. With my dad's help, she and my sister loaded my mom's well-used, aging Maytag washer in the pickup truck and drove it from Ogden to Salt Lake City.

When they arrived, I thanked her for her thoughtfulness but explained that we didn't have any place to put it in our little apartment.

"We'll work something out," she said.

And she did. She worked a miracle.

After looking at the bathroom, she decided there was just enough space between the sink and the door frame to put it against the wall. That left a path of about eight inches between the front of the washer and the bathtub. I pointed out that I had no way to fill it. But she had already considered that problem. She had borrowed two golf tubes from my father's golf bag (which he never got back), and after making sure they would be long enough when joined, she cut two slits in the bottom of one so it would slide into the top of the other. Then she removed the shower head and put the top of the first one over the pipe where it came out of the wall. *Voila!*

To empty the washer, we put the drain hose in the tub. We had to be careful not to kick it out while the washer was pumping the water out, or it would fill our apartment with four inches of water.

Aside from the inconvenience of filling it for the wash cycle and the rinse cycle, my problem appeared solved, except for the little challenge of needing hot water for the diapers. When we used hot water, the tubes softened, collapsed, and gave me a soaking almost as thorough as the laundry needed. It was not uncommon for me to leave the apartment to do the grocery shopping looking as if I had taken my clothing directly from the washer.

Drying the prodigious amount of diapers these boys used, as well as the rest of the laundry, was our next challenge. This was in a day long before most women could take a dryer for granted, so we were happy to locate a space between the wall of the apartment building and the neighbor's fence of about two feet in width. We jury-rigged a clothes line, and I kept it full daily.

This was the system I used for the next two years until we could rent a house with a regular washer hook-up. Wow, I was in heaven when I had a washer in the basement. The boys grew in our care, and eventually, we were permitted to adopt them, but I have always wondered what I would have done if my mother had not been inspired to furnish me with that life-saving washing machine. In all seriousness, I never would have survived.

She has gone through the veil, and there, it is my hope that when we greet each other again, we will laugh about the miracle of the washing machine.

OTHER BOOKS AND AUDIO BOOKS
BY JEAN HOLBROOK MATHEWS

The Light Above

Precious Cargo

The Assignment

Escape to Zion

Safe Haven

Run for Your Life

Showers from Heaven
Margot Hovley

Elder Brandon Smith walked beside his companion down a road filled with craters. Fifteen years ago, war had covered this land. The armies had bombed the roadways as part of some strategy, and all this time later, the roads remained a crazy patchwork of holes, a mute testimony of past conflict. Fixing them wasn't a priority in such a place.

Sierra Leone. A year ago, the missionary had never heard of it. When he read his mission call, he thought perhaps Sierra Leone was a state in Mexico. Instead, he found himself in West Africa.

He looked sidelong at his companion, his first since arriving from the Ghana MTC one month ago. They wore shirtsleeves only, their suits hanging in a closet at the mission home, to be worn just one more time during their missions—on the plane ride home. His companion, Elder Williams, strode confidently around rocks and pits in the road, but Elder Smith thought about that suit in the closet. He wondered how soon he could put it on. Not in twenty-two months. That was too long to endure. He wanted it as soon as possible.

He'd prayed for a hard mission, but this was ridiculous. Yes, Africa lived up to its reputation: mysterious, remote, otherworldly. At first the newness was so engrossing that he forgot to be homesick, but now, he couldn't bear it. The oppressive, damp heat, the bugs crawling through his mosquito netting at night, the long, dark evenings with no electricity in their miserable little shack/house, where he had to use a flashlight to do his scripture study, to find his bed when at last it was time—where he'd lie sweltering instead of sleeping. The bucket outside the door filling with the incessant rain he'd use in the morning to dump over his head for a pseudo shower. The memory of what it was like to turn on a faucet and have hot, clean water pour out at his wish. Soft, fragrant soap. A washing machine. Dryer sheets. High-speed Internet.

He needed to get out.

They didn't need him here anyway. After only a month, he'd discovered that the people in Sierra Leone were flocking to the baptismal font. He'd already baptized more people the first week than his father had his entire European mission. *Anyone could do this*, he thought. *They don't really need me.*

That's what he told himself.

The day before, he'd written his mother an e-mail at a terrible little Internet café. He told her what he knew would break her heart—that he couldn't be the missionary she'd always hoped he'd be. He knew she'd cry, but he wrote it anyway.

He imagined her sitting in their comfortable home, far away in America, clicking open her e-mail. She'd seen his letter only minutes after he'd typed it and had even sent him a message back while he was still at the café.

Hang on. You're not a quitter. I'm praying for you.

But she was wrong. He needed to quit. Now.

Elder Williams walking beside him was patient—a good guy, who was sure things would work themselves out for Elder Smith. But while the companion wasn't looking, the missionary took out the mission-use-only cell phone. Tears mixing with the sweat on his cheeks, he typed a text message.

mom help me please

He held the phone tight, thumb hovering over the send button. He nearly pressed it but slipped it into his pocket instead. Maybe tonight . . .

Maybe tomorrow . . .

Time passed. Elder Smith counted the days until he could speak to the mission president and request to be sent home. In the meantime, he tried to follow the mission rules. He even baptized people, their beautiful dark faces shining as they came out of the river. He knew he should feel that happy suffusion of the Spirit, but all he felt was exhausted, frustrated, and bug-bitten. His mother's prayers didn't seem to be warding off the bugs.

He and Elder Williams traveled to an area they hadn't tracted before, but one muddy, pock-marked road looked like another. As they walked, Elder Williams prayed aloud, "Lead us to the ones searching for truth."

Even before he said amen, they heard a woman calling to them. Looking up, Elder Smith saw her flap her arms urgently in a beckoning gesture. At first he thought there was an emergency of some kind and ran up the rutted path to her side.

"Come, come," she said, waving them into her home—a hut made of sticks.

Inside, her husband sat on the ground on a mat, legs crossed.

"I've been praying for someone to come teach me about the Jesus," he said. "Can you do this?"

Elder Williams assured him that, indeed, they could. After only two days, the man joyfully accepted baptism, his face beaming.

"You don't know how I've longed for this," he said. "Now you are filling me with such happiness. Now my life is wonderful."

Elder Smith looked at the man. He sat on the same mat on the same dirt floor of the same stick house. There was nothing else in the room. How could he think his life was wonderful? He had nothing.

Elder Smith knew deep in his heart that, in reality, the man had *everything*. But he didn't want to admit it. He didn't want to acknowledge that the work he was doing in Africa was important—even life changing. He couldn't face that because then he'd feel compelled to stay, when all he wanted to do was go home.

The two missionaries went into the street to find a ride back to their house. They usually got around by hiring a ride on the back of a scooter, and today would be no different. Scooters of all shapes and sizes zoomed back and forth, and soon, they each had an eager scooter-taxi driver.

Watching his companion's bike speed away, Elder Smith climbed on the back of his ride. The driver took off, deftly swerving around the bombed-out places. Then it started to rain, as it did each afternoon. Water came down in sheets, filling the bomb holes. Mud splattered from the wheels onto their legs.

Elder Smith sighed. Soaked. Again.

He waited for the annoyed feeling to hit him as it always did. One more aggravation on top of a million others. He clenched his teeth, bracing himself for the torrent of negative thought: The heat. The mud. People constantly catcalling and pointing to his blond hair. The food (weird leaf paste and rice three meals a day). The girl he'd left at home.

Tired. I'm so tired.

But suddenly, the rain felt different.

For some reason, when heaven opened with rain this time, it opened in another way. He couldn't explain it, but as the water poured onto his head and shoulders, he felt a hundred prayers wash over him. It was as if they had been held behind a dam that suddenly burst open. He felt every one now. Prayers his mother had prayed on his behalf since the day he left on his mission—no—since the day he was born. A hundred prayers, a thousand prayers, a million prayers rushing over him, filling him, saturating him. The Spirit surged into him so strongly it felt like his chest would ignite.

For a moment, he sensed his mother's arms around him, holding him close. He felt other prayers too—father, grandparents, siblings, relatives of all kinds—and the people of Africa themselves praying for him. He felt them all, and he could no longer deny that he needed to be there in that place. He knew that in that moment, those prayers were being answered.

He turned his face to the sky and let the rain splash.

OTHER BOOKS
BY MARGOT HOVLEY

Sudden Darkness

Glimmering Light

Prayer Will Take You There
Jodi Marie Robinson

STANDING NEXT TO MY COUSIN's tiny grave, my heart ached. I, along with several members of my extended family, had come to pay our respects.

The hot August sun streamed down like a blessing from heaven as my uncle Lamar uttered a prayer of thanks for the circumstances that had brought all of us together. He expressed his appreciation to those who had traveled to be with him and my aunt Yvonne to celebrate and remember their son Randy.

It had been thirty-seven years since a young father and mother buried their six-month-old son after he passed away unexpectedly. His grave was in a small military cemetery in Virginia because, at that time, my uncle was serving in the air force.

After retiring, Aunt Yvonne and Uncle Lamar moved from Virginia to Utah, a distance of 2,200 miles, and not being able to visit Randy's grave on a regular basis was especially disheartening for my aunt. So she began a lengthy process to relocate her son's grave to their local cemetery in Cedar City. They had finally done that, and by choice, my aunt and uncle were reliving the graveside service from so long ago so that, as my aunt so lovingly articulated, they could be "close to him."

She leaned down and set a bouquet of flowers tied with a blue ribbon next to the newly placed gray headstone engraved with a picture of Jesus touching the face of a child. The date read December 1968–July 1969. The expression on my aunt's face as she peered down at her baby's name, Randall Lamar Jordan, told me that having a headstone, after all these years, gave her a sense of needed closure. When Randy died, they could not afford one.

Today's dedication of the grave was brief but meaningful. I imagined my aunt and uncle were pleased being surrounded by their two living children and all of their grandchildren, as well as other family members, as they talked about what a sweet baby Randy had been.

Their daughter Becky, my first cousin, stood next to me during the service. She and I were close, like sisters. She was Randy's fraternal twin, born one minute before he was. Her emotions that day were close to the surface, and my aunt was sensitive to that. So before talking to anyone else, after the dedication ended, my aunt immediately walked over to us, reached out, and hugged her daughter tightly.

At some point, I wrapped my arms around both of them, and then the three of us talked for several minutes about our deep conviction for life after death, how we knew beyond doubt that Randy's spirit was in the spirit world and that he was and always would be part of a forever family.

"Just knowing his final resting place is here gives me great comfort," my aunt said, knowing we would understand what she meant.

It was then that the thought came to me, even though I tried hard to push it away: "If only I had a grave to visit."

I felt it but dared not say it.

A brisk wind rushed against the trees, carrying with it leaves from the full branches. Suddenly, I was reminded of the fragile state I was in. Relieved that no one else could hear my innermost thoughts, I wondered if I should be punished for such thinking.

My mother knew how I felt. But she was the only one. She had called me from her home in Philadelphia the night before I left for Cedar to voice concern that my attending the memorial might stir up fresh memories of my recent loss. When I told her how I felt, it had worried her.

I had recently miscarried at fourteen and half weeks and was still recovering. It was my second miscarriage in nine months, and I was struggling to heal emotionally.

That night, my mom had asked, "Are you sure you feel up to it, because when your father and I visited Randy's grave this past week in Virginia, it was quite an emotional day. I am worried about you."

Since my parents lived in Pennsylvania, my aunt had asked them to go to Virginia to be the witnesses, as required by law, when baby Randy's grave was disinterred—a request no mother should ever have to make, and yet, I could completely understand why she had asked them, and given the circumstances, I knew I would have chosen to do the same.

During our conversation, I assured my mother that Cedar was only a three-hour drive from Riverton and that, although my husband couldn't take time off of work to accompany me and the kids, I knew I would be fine. "I'm actually looking forward to staying the weekend with Becky," I told her. "I should be there for Becky too. That's important."

It was Becky's voice that jarred me back to reality. "Jodi, are you okay?"

In a trance, I was peering down at the grass beneath my feet but finally looked up at her. I felt unsteady. Hoping to hide the panic overcoming me, I took a deep breath and said, "Yes, I'm okay. You go on ahead, and I'll join you in a minute."

For weeks, I had been fearful of thinking about my frantic drive to the hospital, followed by the silent ultrasound that bore witness to my unexpected heartbreak.

I knew she had other family members to talk to, so I urged her to go visit with them. As she turned to walk away, I imagined that her brother Randy would have looked a lot like she did as an adult, with golden-blond hair but blues eyes instead of brown.

After Becky left me, in the August sun, I felt like I was going to dry up and blow away. I didn't want this day to be about me, but it was too late. The circumstances had already broken open my aching heart. I put on my sunglasses to try to hide. I was grateful my three children were busy playing in the grass with their cousins so I wouldn't have to explain to them why Mommy was crying—again.

"Please, Father in Heaven," I pleaded. "Take away my pain. Help me understand."

Hollow was the word I used to describe my mental and physical state. Empty womb. Broken heart. I longed to feel the light and not the darkness that had consumed me for weeks. How my aunt had healed her heart from losing a baby who had lived for six months, I did not know. I did not know how to escape the dark and walk into the light again.

When I had my first miscarriage, nearly a year earlier, I feared that my depressed state would cheat my three other children out of a happy, contented mother who was usually on the go with them 24/7, taking them to the park, the library, the movies, and on rides along the bike path. A year later, another pregnancy had given me hope, and I was happy again. When I made it past six weeks, then eight, then ten and twelve, I became more hopeful each day.

I was impatient to get back to the way things were before I felt broken, and I longed to be whole and emotionally present so I would not miss any precious time with my children, ages eight, five, and three.

That day, deep inside me, I was attending to a baby gone too soon. And because of that, there was a gaping hole, and as much as I tried to fill it, I couldn't.

I stood alone, pleading with Heavenly Father to have pity on me. I knew He wouldn't judge me for wanting closure, and I was so grateful I could share with Him in plain honesty my truest feelings and could trust He would hear my thoughts as I prayed silently.

"Is it wrong, Father, to secretly long for a place, other than my heart, where I could I visit my babies? A place where I could physically mark their existence on this earth? I have learned from firsthand experience that mothers who have miscarriages know of no such place. Still, in me exists a desire to bring flowers and sit on the grass and sing lullabies. Even though I know my babies are in heaven, I want them to be remembered. Am I alone in feeling this way?"

I had come to believe miscarriage was somewhat of a solo journey. A husband, not for lack of trying, didn't really understand what it felt like to have a baby growing inside. How wonderful and exhilarating it felt to be kicked and poked from the inside, to go from feeling a sense of companionship and oneness one moment to a sudden aloneness and emptiness the next.

Right then, the thought, "You are not alone," floated into my mind.

Again, it came. "You are not alone."

I didn't hear anyone speak it. But I sure felt it as real as the sun's rays. At that moment, peace enveloped me from head to toe. And I dared not move.

I knew Heavenly Father had heard me. And I knew He was reminding me that He had never left me alone, especially on that night when I had awakened with severe abdominal pain and recognized that my body was in labor. Having had a miscarriage the previous summer, I understood what it felt like to be losing a baby, and because of the way I was feeling, I knew He was there for me as I panicked at the thought of losing another one.

He had been there in the hospital when I had felt scared and sad, trying to hang on to hope.

He had been there when the nurse had hooked me up to a monitor and had given me an expression I didn't want to see.

He had been there when I asked the doctors: *Did I do something wrong? Did I not eat right? Was I too active?*

He had been there when the doctor reassured me and my husband that the baby growing inside me had not developed the way he should have, so nature was taking its course.

And He had been there when I walked into the nursery with empty arms to stare at an empty crib.

"You *were* not alone." The voice came again. And I was sure it was coming from above.

It was the confirmation I had been waiting for. With it came the same feeling I had experienced in the hospital when my husband had stepped out of the room to find the nurse.

Left alone briefly, I had felt a presence standing next to my hospital bed. I couldn't see it. But I could feel it. I had been in labor for a while and understood what was ahead of me. I had yelled out, "I can't do this!" and then felt someone tell me, "Yes, you can, Mom. I am here."

I remembered a warm touch on my arm, as if someone's hand was being placed there.

What seemed like hours had been only minutes when my husband stepped back into the room. In words broken by my utter amazement of what I had just experienced, I tried telling him that I had just felt the presence of an angel. I was not sure he completely believed me.

When the doctor returned, I overheard her telling my husband my body wanted to be pregnant so badly and that it was just not letting go.

That was true! I wanted to be pregnant. I wanted my baby!

I remembered that my body, though aching, had felt as if it was filled with light. That angelic presence stayed with me and kept me strong into the wee hours of the morning and, I believe, finally helped me let go.

Up until that day in the cemetery, I had wondered if what I had felt in the hospital was real. My emotional state, not to mention hormones in the ensuing weeks, had made me question the validity of the experience and caused the sweetness to sour.

That day, at Randy's graveside service, Heavenly Father was giving me a confirmation that He indeed had never left me alone. He had given me a gift.

I understood that my mind had been clear that night in the hospital, that I had been awake and alert and that I had not been dreaming. I clearly understood that the gift I had received was real—to feel heavenly joy in the midst of mortal sorrow. I knew one thing for sure: I had found my sacred place, and it was only a prayer away.

The sound of sweet laughter jolted me back to the present as the wind shifted directions.

I watched relatives climb into their cars to drive to my aunt and uncle's home.

The dedication of the grave was complete.

My youngest son pulled on my leg. I smiled at his blond, curly hair, which was a mystery to me and my husband because we were both part Italian and had dark brown hair. I picked my son up, squeezed him, and told him it was time to go.

I suddenly wanted to feel the sun on my face and see the beauty of the day. I took off my sunglasses and tucked them into my purse. As I peered down at the flowers and wreathes placed on the grave, an unexpected closure filled my being.

I would never forget him—my son. And I knew God would not forget any of us. He knew me. And He knew every child who did and would come into existence, no matter how briefly.

At my aunt's home that afternoon, the caring and concern I saw exchanged between family members encircled me as well. And I felt so grateful to be reminded of the beauty of believing in an eternal family.

My babies were part of that eternal family. I was blessed to know that.

That day, my bitterness tasted sweet. It was a sure sign that healing had begun; it offered me reassurance that the peace I was seeking would come in time as long as I continued to reach toward heaven.

I am so grateful for a Heavenly Father who understands a mother's grief and her odd request to have a sacred place to remember her son. I know now there is such a place, and I can carry it with me in my heart. Whenever I am missing my babies, I know prayer will take me to them.

OTHER BOOKS
BY JODI MARIE ROBINSON

A Royal Guardian

Precious in His Sight

My Mother's Wedding Dress
Michele Ashman Bell

As I MADE THE FOUR-HOUR drive from my house in the Salt Lake Valley to Southern Utah to visit my mom and dad, I fought back tears. This wasn't the way things were supposed to happen. My mom, who had been vibrant, healthy, and active all her life, had Alzheimer's.

My father, three sisters, and I had known for a while that something wasn't right. Mom began to forget important things, like birthdays and holidays; she became more withdrawn and uncomfortable in family gatherings, and she struggled to carry on a conversation and forgot simple things.

None of us wanted to face the reality of what we secretly feared. Physically, she was fine, but mentally, she was losing the ability to perform simple everyday tasks. Worse, though, was that she was losing touch with things that had been vitally important to her—mainly, her family.

The diagnosis of this disease was a difficult and bitter pill to swallow. The word *Alzheimer's* took away any hope that she could recover. My heart broke for my father, who had just retired. Their golden years together would be tarnished with the reality of this cruel disease and the challenges the future held.

For me, one of the most difficult trials of our earthly existence is watching a loved one suffer. It's painful to know that we can't step in to take it away or go through it for them, but I am strengthened by and very grateful for the knowledge that Heavenly Father hears and answers prayers and that He is aware of us.

My mother gave me that knowledge. She was always an example of unwavering faith and exemplified her testimony of the gospel and love for the Savior. It didn't matter what trials came her way, she received strength to face them through her deep-rooted beliefs and knowledge of eternal truths. For her, prayer was the answer for everything. I learned of her testimony of prayer through her example. No matter how big or small the problem, prayer was the best solution.

It is her example of faith and prayer that has helped me as I've faced difficult and sometimes overwhelming trials in my own life.

Yet as I went to visit my mother and my sweet father, I struggled to feel peace and comfort about the situation. I wanted to know this was all part of God's plan. I prayed desperately that I'd find a connection with her, a tiny glimmer of recognition in her eyes when she saw me. I prayed that somehow, behind the blank expression in her eyes, some small part of the wonderful woman who had raised me would emerge.

Upon my arrival, I gave her a hug, then knelt down in front of her, took her hands, and looked into her eyes. "Hi, Mom; it's me, Michele, your daughter."

I searched her eyes, praying that a spark would ignite and that she'd remember. I wanted so desperately to have her back, if only for a brief moment. And I mentally kicked myself for not spending more time with her when she was well. Over and over, I asked myself why I hadn't found out every possible thing about her life while she could still tell me. All the personal stories of her childhood, teen years, and adulthood were stored away behind the fog that hid her memories. I used the precious gift of prayer she had given me yet again to ask for a small miracle during this visit to make the connection with her I so desperately wanted.

My three sisters joined me at our parents' house, something we decided to do on a regular basis now. When we were together, the heaviness of the situation seemed a little easier to endure. Their presence brought comfort and peace and strength. We always ended up reminiscing about our years growing up together; we laughed, and we cried, grateful to have each other.

During our visit, our reminiscing turned to Mom's cedar chest and how one of our favorite things to do when we were younger was coax our mother into opening her cedar chest so we could look through the treasures she kept in there—items she'd saved from her childhood, teen years, and early married years as a young wife and mother. She was never one to talk a lot about herself or draw attention to herself, so we had to pester and beg her to tell us stories associated with the items. One of the most treasured possessions was her beautiful lace-covered wedding dress, still surprisingly white and in perfect condition since she'd worn it on her wedding day in the St. George Temple back in April 1956. The vintage style was reminiscent of the fifties, with a tight-fitted bodice, lacy long sleeves, and a scallop-edged neckline. The tea-length skirt had yards of fabric, but it was the crinoline petticoat and stiff layers of netting that made it billow out, full and elegant. Sometimes she would let my sisters and me try on the dress, and we would take pictures and imagine ourselves on our own special wedding day in the future when we would enter the temple to be sealed for eternity.

After we were done, she would carefully fold the dress and place it lovingly back into the cedar chest. She even still had the advertisement of it from a fashion magazine back in her day. I loved the style and classy elegance of the clothes from that era and sometimes wished I had been born sooner so I could wear the gorgeous, glamorous dresses Doris Day, Audrey Hepburn, and Grace Kelly wore in the movies my mother and I watched together.

On this particular day, as we lifted the lid, right on top of everything, we found her school sweater. We coaxed Mom to stand up so we could take pictures of her wearing it, and we smiled because it seemed to make her happy. We looked at old photographs and other mementos that had special meaning to her, and then we pulled out her wedding dress. Seeing it again reminded me of my childhood and the fun my sisters and I had growing up together. It also reminded me of my mom as a young woman with dreams of her own as she began her life with my father and of the covenants of the temple and the sealing power that binds families together for eternity.

As my sisters and I talked about the dress and the memories we recalled, we compared the actual dress to the picture from the magazine and asked our dad details about where the dress had been purchased or if it had been ordered from a catalogue. Out of the blue, my mother said in a quiet voice, "I made it."

We all stopped talking and looked at her in wonder. With further discussion and asking a lot of yes and no questions, we found out my mother had clipped the picture out of a magazine and had made the dress herself to look like the one she had found. On closer inspection, we could tell that in the fine stitches and tiny details of lace-covered buttons running up the back, the carefully appliquéd scallops of lace around the neckline, and the painstaking finishing of seams, it was indeed our sweet mother's handiwork. All this time and all these years, we had thought the dress was store-bought, only to find out she had worked long and hard to make the dress for her wedding. Knowing she made it with her own hands made it even more special.

A wave of emotion came over me, and I said a small prayer of thanks for the tender mercy we received that allowed us to share one special moment with our mom, a moment we knew might never happen again.

Through the personal trials I've had in my own family, watching my sweet mother deal with Alzheimer's and my wonderful father take such loving care of her, I have learned to never take the people I love for granted. Now is when we need to cherish the time we have with them, and now is when we should absorb and record every special experience from their lives.

I am who I am today because of my mother. Every good quality I have is because of her. Her life, her example has given me a template of how I should live my life. She is a noble, elect woman as described in the scriptures.

To paraphrase Proverbs: "Who can find a virtuous woman? for her price is far above rubies. . . . She . . . worketh willingly with her hands. . . . With the fruit of her hands she planteth a vineyard. . . . She stretcheth out her hand to the poor. . . . Strength and honour are her clothing. . . . She openeth her mouth with wisdom; and in her tongue is the law of kindness. She looketh well to the ways of her household, and eateth not the bread of idleness" (31:10, 13, 16, 20, 25–27).

I am grateful for my mother, who taught me well and sacrificed greatly so I could know the importance of the gospel, of faith and prayer, and of the covenants that make our family eternal.

OTHER BOOKS AND AUDIO BOOKS
BY MICHELE ASHMAN BELL

Timeless Moments series

Yesterday's Love series

Butterfly Box series

A Candle in the Window

The Value of Motherhood
Sandra Grey

"I HATE MOTHER'S DAY." SARA wouldn't look at me. I was shocked at my friend's words as I stared at her, trying to make sense of the emotion. We stood in my kitchen, and the warm afternoon sun filtered through the curtains into the room, emphasizing the dishes still in my sink. Sara leaned against the counter, holding her eight-month-old son and absently playing with his toes. The baby reached out and grabbed at a lock of her hair as she cuddled him. I broke half a banana into a bowl. Beside me, my firstborn daughter banged on her high chair with a spoon. "Na-Na!" she insisted, eyes locked on the fruit in my hand. I added milk and rice cereal to the bowl and then pureed the mixture with a fork. I was concerned by my friend's revelation, and I could think of nothing more than generic words of sympathy to offer in the face of such a surprising admission.

"I didn't always hate Mother's Day . . ." Sara's voice trailed off, and she finally looked at me. She must have caught the look on my face—the look I couldn't mask in time that said, *Who hates Mother's Day?* She dropped her eyes, focusing her attention on her son. I waited, frustrated at myself for hurting her and wishing she would continue to confide in me.

She didn't. She lifted her chin, forced a smile, and changed the subject. She didn't bring it up again. But I pondered her words, and I wondered about the obvious anxiety in her voice as she'd said them. I couldn't understand how anyone could hate Mother's Day—especially a mother.

My husband and I later moved far away. I had a second child. And I thought about Sara often. I eventually called her, and she cried over the phone as she told me her marriage was falling apart. Over the next few months, she told me about her husband's addictions, his abuse. She told me of his eventual affair and how hard she'd tried to make things work, tried to make him want to stay. But he finally left anyway.

I didn't know how to deal with it. I told her I was so sorry, that it must be difficult being a single mom. I said all the comforting things I could think of while at the same time struggling to understand a tragedy impossible for me to comprehend. We talked often, and before we hung up each time, we always promised to keep in touch. But I was busy. I taught violin lessons and helped my husband start a business.

And because of Sara's awful tragedy, I downplayed the subtle hints of trouble in my own marriage and worked harder to be a better wife and mother.

We had another baby and moved again. My husband began working near the New Mexico border, and the business he and I had established continued to flourish on the side. He was constantly gone, working, working. Financially, he took good care of our family. But he was gone a lot, and when he was home, he seemed distant.

I took care of our business and our growing family, and my life became so hectic that after a few years, Sara and her tragedy faded out of my life. Unfortunately, entire chapters of my existence passed without me giving my faraway friend much thought. And then after sixteen years of wedlock, my own marriage exploded into oblivion. I stood by like a stunned survivor and watched as everything I had hoped and dreamed for was destroyed in the blast. I found myself suddenly living a life I'd vowed I would never experience; I could recall several times in my past where news of some celebrity marriage falling apart had made me judgmental and self-righteous. I came from a wonderful, spiritually strong family, where the word *divorce* had no valid definition. Now, that word defined *me*.

I was so grateful that my own family was supportive and kind, but my own disappointment and disorientation allowed self-doubt and sadness to erode me into a shell of my former self. I became that person at church who smiles on the outside while she cries on the inside.

And then my first Mother's Day as a suddenly single mother loomed. I thought again about Sara. I finally understood how she could hate Mother's Day. I finally understood the trauma that can make the universal connection of *wife* and *mother* painful and can cause a woman to link her own self-worth to married motherhood.

I gave Sara a call. We talked for a long time. She listened, let me cry on her digital shoulder, let me explain how I finally understood her words from that sunny afternoon in my kitchen so long ago.

"Oh, but I don't hate Mother's Day," she murmured. "Not anymore."

I hesitated, confused.

"It was tough," she said. "It's still tough. But my mother gave me a challenge when I was new at all this, back when I was raw and wounded—like you are right now."

"What sort of challenge?"

"To look outside my own grief and make Mother's Day special for someone else."

It sounded too simple. Too juvenile. And then, at the same time, it sounded impossible. Sure, I'd been taught my entire life that service was supposed to help me feel better. But this hurt ran so deep, was so intertwined with the workings of my heart and soul that I couldn't see that it would make any difference in the way I hurt.

"It works, Sandra. You should try it."

My life was a frenzied spectacle of children, school, job search, custody issues, empty bank accounts, insensitive bill collectors, and sleepless, lonely, anxious nights. The thought of adding one more thing to the mix made me physically ill. But as Mother's Day approached, I found myself on my knees more than once asking God, hesitantly, if there was anything I could do to help another woman feel her worth as a mother. And if possible, could I feel mine too?

The day before Mother's Day, I muscled my three youngest into the car. I had a shopping list bigger than my bank account and a list of errands twice as long as my available time motivating me to hurry.

The oldest of the three wailed that he didn't want to go. I was surprised; he was usually the first out the door whenever he caught wind of a road trip. But this time, he resisted my efforts to strap him down in his car seat, and I realized I was not in the mood for a battle. I released him and let him stay home with his older siblings.

I slipped into the driver's seat and headed toward town with my two youngest in tow. My three-year-old spread his arms and made airplane sounds as I drove past warm-cut alfalfa fields, the scent of late spring making its way into the van. Cornfields planted in military-perfect rows stretched as far as the eye could see on my left, and on the right, cherry and apple orchards beckoned with promises of soothing shade. But my preoccupation with current events kept me from appreciating the beauty of the countryside that was my new home.

I also didn't notice the young woman walking alongside the road, mammoth diaper bag on one arm and toddler in the other. But sometimes God has a way of piercing through the layers of worry and stress that envelope me and bringing those things to my attention.

In this case, it took almost a mile for the image of the woman and child to penetrate. I applied the brakes, slowing to a crawl. I turned around in the middle of the road and drove back.

My three-year-old's airplane sputtered, slowed. "Mommy, what are we doing?" He knew I had deviated from my flight plan.

"I'm just going to talk to that lady, all right?"

"Why?"

"Because I think she needs our help."

"Are we going to help her?"

"If she wants us to."

I turned again and pulled up alongside the woman, realizing as I did so that any sane, careful person might think the worst of me for stopping. My cheeks went warm, and I suddenly felt like an axe murderer ready to corner her next victim.

She had been crying. She turned away and wiped madly at her eyes when she saw me.

I rolled down the window. "Do you need any help?"

She hesitated, wary, I'm sure, of the offer and the remote location. And then my three-year-old began singing a children's song from his car seat. "I want to be kind to everyone, for that is right, you see . . ."

The woman glanced back, saw him and his baby sister, and relaxed. "My car broke down," she offered. "I have a job interview in an hour, and I have to get my baby to daycare so I can catch the bus."

"Where's daycare?" I asked and felt a little less like an axe murderer.

"Other side of the freeway." She hefted the toddler on her hip.

"Can I give you a ride?"

Again, she hesitated.

"I'm new here," I said, trying to reassure her, feeling awkward again. "My name's Sandra, and I just moved in." I pointed up the hill. "See? That's my house, the one with the green roof."

Her eyes followed to where I was pointing and then turned back to analyze me.

"I have an extra car seat." I added one last perk to the offer, and when she still hesitated, I realized I hadn't felt that awkward in a long time. In fact, I wouldn't have thought worse of her for refusing my offer. "Listen"—I cleared my throat—"I can understand if you would prefer not—"

"I have three miles to walk," she said. "I really could use the ride. Thank you."

I don't remember her name. But I remember that as we talked, I learned she was a newly single mother, like me, confronting much of the same uncertainty and fear I was facing. We reached her destination, and she unbuckled her toddler, grabbed her bag, and stepped onto the curb.

"Thanks," she said and moved to close the van door.

I leaned toward her. "Happy Mother's Day," I blurted through the door and felt a little foolish.

She stared at me, speechless, and I managed an embarrassed grin. "Tomorrow's Mother's Day, you know."

She glanced down at her baby. "You're the only one who's ever said that to me," she mumbled. "Sometimes I don't feel much like a mother . . ."

"You're a great mother," I said and suddenly felt more that way myself. My smile widened, and she finally met it with her own tentative smile.

As I drove away, I felt a warm, pleasant sensation begin at the pit of my stomach and radiate outward until it warmed me all the way to my fingertips. I could hardly wait to call Sara to tell her. And I couldn't help but wonder if it had been a kind and loving Father in Heaven who had made my son so determined to stay home so a woman who needed me could use the car seat for her baby. The experience made me feel valuable, needed. And I realized that I had been praying for just such a feeling.

My load was not any lighter, my future not any more secure, but the idea that I was just as valid a mother without the blessing of a husband currently at my side had begun to work its way into my soul. I realized I wanted to believe it. I wanted to *feel* it. And perhaps this Mother's Day I was one step closer to knowing it was true.

OTHER BOOKS AND AUDIO BOOKS
BY SANDRA GREY

Traitor

Tribunal

Trespass

Trolley Square
Karen Tuft

*On the evening of February 12, 2007, eighteen-year-old Sulejman
Talović armed himself with a shotgun, a handgun, and a backpack full of
ammunition and then went to Trolley Square in Salt Lake City to engage
in a shooting spree. An hour later, six people were dead from gunshot
wounds, including Talović himself, and four others were critically wounded.*

*Among those wounded was my husband's sister Carolyn Tuft. Her
daughter Kirsten Hinckley—my fifteen-year-old niece and the youngest
victim—was one of those who died.*

IT WASN'T A TYPICAL MONDAY evening to begin with. My husband,
Stephen, called to say he'd be working late. My oldest daughter,
Lauren, and my son, Stewart, had recently left on missions. Sixteen-
year-old Rebecca had been working on a group school project and was
at a friend's house. That left me at home with my sixth grader, Holly.

As I threw our meal together, I flipped on the TV. But instead of the
regular programming I'd expected, every channel was running breaking
news about a shooting at Trolley Square. And it was literally breaking
news—the shooting was still occurring. The images were gripping: people
scrambling, reporters dashing about and updating their information live,
emergency vehicles and police cars arriving with flashing lights and
sirens blaring. Speculations. SWAT teams taking position.

I called Stephen to warn him that something bad was happening at
Trolley Square and to be careful when he left work to come home. Then
I went back to following the news as it unfolded. Holly and I were glued
to the TV.

At around eight o'clock, the shooting appeared to be over. Police
were scouring the area for casualties. Emergency crews were attending

the wounded. There was a TV image of a woman on a gurney. Holly commented that the boot the woman wore looked like one of Aunt Carolyn's "spider boots," nicknamed because they had pointed toes and Carolyn joked that it was so she could get spiders in the corners of rooms with them. The image of the woman on the gurney haunted me.

As we continued watching and trying to make sense of it all, the telephone rang. Holly answered it and then handed the phone to me. A man identified himself as a representative of LDS Hospital and asked if he'd reached the Stephen Tuft residence. When I answered in the affirmative, he asked if he could speak to Stephen. I told him he wasn't home. The man paused and then asked if Stephen had any sisters.

An uneasy feeling swept over me.

Answering yes to his question, I proceeded to rattle off the names of Stephen's two oldest sisters before my mind went completely blank.

The man asked if Stephen had any other sisters.

I'd completely forgotten to tell him about Carolyn, even after the spider-boot comment. "Yes, Carolyn," I said.

"That's the one," he replied.

The uneasy feeling got worse.

"Is Carolyn at the hospital?" I asked. "What's going on? Is she okay?"

He said he wasn't at liberty to say anything other than to tell me she was there and she was in critical condition.

With that comment, my sense of foreboding went into overdrive. "Look," I told him, "I've been watching the news all evening, and I've seen what's going on at Trolley Square. Does this have anything to do with that?"

"Yes," he answered and ended the call.

Carolyn had been the woman on the gurney.

Sickened, I immediately called Stephen. "Remember what I told you about Trolley Square?" I said. "Carolyn was one of the people shot there, and she's at LDS Hospital right now."

He told me he'd call his siblings immediately and head up to the hospital to find out what was going on.

Holly and I continued to watch the TV for additional news, and I waited for the telephone to ring.

At around nine o'clock, Stephen finally called. I could tell by his voice that it was bad before he even told me what he knew. "Carolyn's in surgery right now," he said, "and they don't know if she'll survive or not. And," he added, "Kirsten was at Trolley too, and they don't think she made it."

Kirsten, my blonde-haired, beautiful niece.

My heart broke, even as I fought not to believe it.

The layers of grief were overwhelming and instant: My own grief at suffering a personal loss. The grief for a husband, who could lose the little sister he'd teased growing up. Grief for my mother- and father-in-law and Kirsten's aunts and uncles and cousins. Grief for Kirsten's father and her siblings. I grieved for Carolyn. I couldn't imagine anything worse than what she had experienced and had yet to face if she survived.

My next thought was, *How am I going to get my children through this?*

As their mother, I *had* to take care of them and help them get through an ordeal they didn't even know about yet. But I wasn't sure how I was going to get through it myself.

And so I prayed.

It was a long and agonizing night. I explained to Holly what had happened. She cried. I cried. I pulled her onto my lap, along with several stuffed animals, and we cuddled, and we waited.

Rebecca came home a short time later. I sat her down at the kitchen table and told her as gently as I could what I knew. Rebecca and Kirsten were the same age and had been inseparable growing up, with countless sleepovers and bubble baths and play dates at Grandma's. The last few years, they'd become estranged though, as teens do as they define who they are and their interests diverge. I didn't know how she would handle the news.

She sobbed, and I held her close and cried some more. It was terrible.

Stephen didn't arrive home until three in the morning, but he had news: Carolyn had survived surgery, but she wasn't out of the woods yet. And the medical examiner had officially identified Kirsten as one of the deceased.

We tried to get a few hours of sleep, but sleep didn't come easily.

The next day we were thrown into a maelstrom. We needed to be at the hospital, to be together there as an extended family. There were phone calls telling us which hospital entrances to use to avoid the media. Everyone was in shock. People were distraught. Doctors and hospital administrators came and went constantly. We were asked to assign a spokesman who would address the media on the family's behalf. The governor and his wife were expected at any moment to offer condolences, and we were told to stand by for instructions for when that occurred. The entire day felt surreal.

Previous personal experience had helped me understand that there was no way any of us could fully prepare for the death of a loved one. But I will state for the record that there was absolutely *no way* to prepare for how a public tragedy like the one at Trolley Square and its aftermath would affect our family personally.

This was further complicated for me by the fact that my four children had never experienced the loss of a loved one before—Lauren had been barely five and Stewart two when my own father had peacefully passed away.

I knew deep down that my most important responsibility was to help my children cope with this tragedy and Kirsten's death. But how was I supposed to do this? How could I understand what my children would individually be going through? Even if I asked them, would they tell me what they were feeling? Would they be able to put those feelings into words? And how was I supposed to help my two children who were away from home serving missions? Who would be there to hold them and make sure they were going to be all right?

I would do everything I could, but they would need more help than I could give them to get through this tragedy.

And so I prayed for my children.

A mother prays for her children from the moment she knows she's conceived until her last dying breath—and possibly even beyond that. It doesn't matter if her child is six days old, six years, or sixty, she will pray for that child.

Most prayers a mother offers are not given immediate answers. There are those times when the miracles happen and the cause and effect of prayers are obvious, but most of the time, a mother has no way of knowing if or how her prayers are being answered. It takes faith and hope that her prayers are being heard.

In the meantime, we keep on praying.

In the midst of family meetings with doctors and administrators and hugs from Governor and Mrs. Huntsman, we called two mission presidents and broke the news to two heartbroken missionaries.

The weeks that followed were tough ones, I cannot lie. It took Carolyn a month and multiple surgeries to be well enough to leave the hospital. In the meantime, there were candlelight vigils and public memorial services and a funeral to prepare for. We had to go back to work, and my girls had to go back to school.

But I had seen enough answers to my prayers during that time to trust that God was watching over my children. And eventually, we learned to accept this new version of life.

The events of Trolley Square are never very far away, though it's been several years now. The world has seen similar tragedies unfold and then has moved on and directed its interest elsewhere. But for those personally affected by this and the other tragedies, life is never the same again.

Even for a mere aunt and sister-in-law.

It took the decision to now write about Trolley Square and to reflect on the prayers I offered for my children during that time to finally ask each of them what they remembered, how they felt, and if they thought God had been watching over them.

I learned there were immediate answers to my prayers as well as long-term blessings.

I learned the answers and blessings were tailor-made for each child.

My son, Stewart, was serving in an area several hours away from the mission office and received the news by phone from his president while he watched his new companion unpack. Then he called us, distraught, and we did everything we could long-distance to comfort him. I was concerned he would be grieving alone, but a kind branch president checked on him frequently, and the branch members rallied around him.

Stewart realized that as a missionary, what he was teaching was essential for families to be together in the eternities, and his heart ached for family members who had that knowledge yet chose not to follow the gospel.

The scope of the tragedy also took him to spiritual depths he may not have reached otherwise.

He focused on studying the plan of salvation. He told me missionaries often become identified by the gospel principle they bear strong testimony about and that he was the missionary people recognized as the one who taught about the plan of salvation. Kirsten's death was the first of thirteen Stewart encountered during his mission, and he was prepared to explain, empathize, and testify in a way he wouldn't have been able to otherwise. I don't believe this was a coincidence.

When the tragedy broke, my daughter Lauren's mission president invited her and her companion to his home for a "Valentine's party," which they thought was strange. He broke the news personally to her and had her call us. Then he and his wife kept Lauren and her companion at their home overnight. This is her experience, in her own words:

The night we stayed in the mission home, I couldn't sleep. I waited until I thought Sister Cameron was asleep and then I prayed. It's one of the moments I remember most vividly. I knelt, and I closed my eyes and tried to think of a prayer, but I couldn't even think of words. In my mind, I uttered, "Heavenly Father—" But then I just lost it. I just sat there midprayer trying to stifle sobs. I felt very distinctly the words "I know. I know." People talk about feeling the Spirit like a hug—I've only felt that once, and it was that night. It's the closest I've ever felt to my Heavenly Father. I knew He knew everything, and I didn't have to say anything.

The next day was another miracle that demonstrated God was orchestrating the details of my life at that time. President Layton told us we were not expected to go out and work like normal for a while. He told me I could take a day or two off if I needed. We drove back to our apartment in the morning. I tried to take a nap, but all I could think of was Sister Cameron being cooped up with me in our apartment not working, and it was my fault. I kept thinking, What good am I doing by sitting here? I couldn't change things. As much as I felt like the world should stop, it wouldn't. And I was still a missionary. I felt guilty sitting at home crying when I was on the Lord's time. I told Sister Cameron we should go out. She was wary and tried to convince me it was okay for me to take some time, but I insisted. Then we got another phone call from President. It had started snowing on our drive home and had gotten much worse since then. President called an official snow day and told all missionaries not to go out. (And yes, the call was made to all missionaries and not just my companionship.) It was the only snow day of my entire mission. I got to have the day off and not feel guilty about not working— it was a huge relief. It allowed me to really have an emotional recovery day. It was more than a tender mercy.

My twelve-year-old, Holly, was the youngest member of the entire extended family, and I was worried about her ability to cope with the tragedy at such a young age. A sensitive elementary school principal, teacher, and counselor all stepped up to the plate, prepared Holly's classmates, and eased the way for her to return to some normalcy and routine.

I was especially concerned for Rebecca. She and Kirsten had had a special bond, and Rebecca had ached for a long time over their estrangement. The Friday night a week before the shooting, we had stopped by Carolyn's home. Kirsten had been there with friends and had invited Rebecca to join them while they delivered cookies to some boys. Because of the distance that had grown between them, Rebecca hadn't felt comfortable and had declined Kirsten's invitation.

Ten days later, Kirsten was dead, and Rebecca had deep, sorrowful regrets that she hadn't taken the opportunity to spend that time with her.

And then the dreams occurred.

A couple of months after the shooting, Holly and Rebecca discovered they'd had similar dreams the same night.

In Holly's dream, she and Rebecca were sitting at the kitchen table when the phone rang. Holly looked at the caller ID; it said it was Rebecca's cell phone calling, which was upstairs in Rebecca's bedroom. Holly got scared, since no one was upstairs at the time. She crept up the stairs, looked in Rebecca's room, and saw Kirsten on Rebecca's phone. Kirsten smiled at Holly, and immediately, Holly's scared feelings left and were replaced by loving, peaceful ones. Then she woke up.

In Rebecca's dream, she and Holly were also sitting at the kitchen table when they heard a noise. They turned around to look.

Kirsten was standing by the entrance to the kitchen, but she wasn't the fifteen-year-old Kirsten who'd lost her life. She was a younger version, one who was very familiar to Rebecca, the one who had been her best cousin-buddy. Kirsten wore khaki shorts and a light-blue T-shirt, and her hair was in a messy ponytail. Rebecca walked over to her and hugged her, and Rebecca immediately felt a warm, loving feeling that told her Kirsten loved her, that she was okay, and that everything was good between them.

What an amazing experience for my two youngest daughters to share. What a blessing.

Stewart testified to many of the plan of salvation. Lauren felt God's arms around her when her mother's couldn't be. Rebecca got to hug her cousin. And Holly told me Trolley Square was when she knew she didn't have to rely on her parents' testimony of the gospel because she knew for herself for the first time that it was true.

Lauren stated it best. She said Trolley Square was a "line drawn in the sand" moment, one of those experiences we face in life that is of such a magnitude that the line is drawn: Do we believe or don't we? How do we choose to proceed? How does it define us?

When the shooting occurred, my mortal motherly concerns were immediate, and they dealt with the finite issues of grief and consolation. And as a companion, Heavenly Father heard my concerns, listened to my prayers, and then generously offered His answers and blessings to my children on a much greater and eternal level than I could have asked or hoped for. Each of my children's specific needs was met in a way even I as their mother hadn't comprehended they needed—or would receive. Each prayer I'd offered for them was answered. They were answered immediately, in the weeks that followed, and in the years since, even though I didn't know they'd been answered.

That's the way it is with most prayers mothers offer.

And mothers will always keep praying.

I know I will.

OTHER BOOKS
BY KAREN TUFT

Reality Check

Unexpected

Answers to Mothers' Prayers
Stephanie Dibb Sorensen

IN A RECENT GENERAL CONFERENCE, President Boyd K. Packer said, "There are few things more powerful than the faithful prayers of a righteous mother."[1] As a mother myself, I loved his apostolic claim. It felt true when he said it, but the more I've reflected on it, the more I've seen evidence in my own life that has strengthened my testimony of mothers' prayers.

I served a mission in Argentina. My second area was a small town called Candelaria, where the red dirt roads dotted with humble homes wandered through the lush green foliage of the Misiones province. I loved Candelaria. The town was small enough that I knew most of its inhabitants by the time I'd spent several months there. My companion, Hermana Dornelles, and I were familiar with all the streets and pathways and felt quite at home in our little town.

One day as we finished our evening visits, we started our journey home. It was not an excessively long walk, but since night had fallen and there were no streetlights, we made our way slowly through the tree-lined pathways in the darkness. We chatted casually and reminisced about our day. We made plans for the next day and talked about the families we had met. At one point, I realized we were walking near the northwest corner of the town, where there was a state-run prison by the river. I didn't feel any fear and even chuckled to think we were wandering by a prison in the dark night, and I said to my companion, "If my mom could see me right now, she would die of worry." We both laughed off the imagined danger and continued on our way until we were safely home.

Only recently did it occur to me that maybe the reason we felt so safe was not that we were so accustomed to the kind of situations that would have made our mothers cringe but perhaps that it was their prayers that kept us safe and confident in situations that might have been dangerous.

On another occasion, while serving in a different area, my companion, Hermana Diaz, and I knelt in prayer before leaving our apartment after the traditional siesta break in our daily schedule. Normally, we used the break for companion and personal study, but after finishing our morning visits and eating a humbly prepared but digestionally challenged meal and then walking almost an hour in the blazing sun, we both found ourselves ill and exhausted. We fell asleep when we should have been studying and woke up with a start several hours after we should have left the apartment. We realized our mistake and hurried to ready ourselves for an appointment with a family who was expecting us. It was already dark, and our destination required a long walk there and back.

Knowing we were overdue to resume our work, we knelt on the concrete floor in the front room and offered our departure prayer. As Hermana Diaz prayed, an image of our intended pathway came into my mind, and I felt uneasy. We had walked that path many times for many weeks, so I brushed off my apprehension and tried to pay attention to the rest of the prayer. We got off our knees, reached for our backpacks, and walked to the door. As I reached out my hand to open the door, the warning feeling returned, and I froze. I stood there silently, just long enough for my pause to be obvious and awkward, and then I turned around and said, "I don't know why, but I feel scared."

"Me too!" blurted out Hermana Diaz.

We looked at each other and knew we weren't supposed to leave our apartment that night. Neither one of us knew why. We just knew to stay put. We sang a few hymns, finished our companionship study, and went to bed early.

I still don't know why we were warned that night. I imagine there was some kind of danger. As I look back, I can also imagine that somewhere, thousands of miles away, my mother probably also knelt in prayer like she did many times each day. Her words probably repeated a familiar plea, "Please bless Stephanie in Argentina. Protect her from harm and keep her safe. Help her to listen to the promptings of the Holy Ghost and be led where to go. Please bring her safely home."

Perhaps no one understands a mother's love more than our Heavenly Parents. And maybe that's why Elder Holland promised mothers their prayers will be heard:

"Be believing. Keep loving and keep testifying. Keep praying. Those prayers will be heard and answered in the most unexpected hour. God will send aid to no one more readily than He will send it to a child— and to the parent of a child."[2]

After my mission, I had several years of dating still ahead of me. As any young single adult can attest, those years are full of angst, adventure, and frustration, and like any stage in life, they are best navigated with prayer. I could have saved myself from some really awkward dating situations with a little bit of dishonesty, but unfortunately, I was never very good at fibbing my way out of unwelcome invitations.

I once went on a date with someone I didn't know very well, and even though it was mostly uneventful, I could tell he was more interested than I was. I knew I didn't want a second date, and while my normal strategy for these situations was avoidance, this time, he caught me off guard.

I was alone at my apartment one evening when the phone rang. I answered it, and he said, "What are you doing right now?"

This is where lying would have come in handy. "Just watching TV," I said.

"I'm taking you out to dinner," he said. "I'll be there in a few minutes."

As I hung up the phone, that familiar warning feeling came. Over time, I've named it "the yuck," and after his call, it hit me in full force. I felt so worried that I called my mom and explained the situation and my feelings. She was concerned for me and probably felt helpless from the other side of the country. She told me to say a prayer and promised to pray for me as well.

I hung up and immediately dropped to my knees in the hallway. I prayed for guidance, wisdom, and safety. As I prayed, I remembered I had two boxes I needed to take to my grandparents' house an hour away. I jumped up, called my younger brother, and asked if he would help me deliver the boxes in a couple hours. He was a college student as well and probably had his own Saturday night plans, but when I explained why I needed him, he understood and agreed.

My unplanned date arrived at the door. As we got into his car, I explained that my brother and I were expected at my grandparents' home, so I would need to be back by eight thirty.

He seemed irritated and said, "I only get you for two and half hours?"

"Sorry about that," I said, but I really wasn't sorry, so I guess I *did* lie a little bit. I felt relieved that this would all be over soon. We went to Olive Garden and ordered dinner. Most of his conversation was inappropriate, and he kept rubbing my leg under the table with his foot. I felt uncomfortable, and my stomach grew unsettled. We were almost finished with our meal when I jumped up and ran to the bathroom.

After several minutes, I returned to the table and told him I was sick and had thrown up. He offered to complain to the manager about the food, but I knew that was not the reason for my illness. We walked out to the car, and as we pulled out of the parking lot, he asked me if I wanted to see a movie. Surprised, I told him I'd better go home.

"But I get you until eight thirty," he insisted.

I said I felt like I was going to throw up again, but instead of pulling over, he sped through the parking lot and pulled behind the large strip mall. I jumped out of the car, crossed the curb, and started pacing the length of the thin strip of grass. By this point, it was obvious that my apprehensive feeling was justified, but as he sat on the curb for the next hour or so and tried to make conversation with me, it became more and more clear. He said things that revealed a violent and self-satisfying character, and I felt so grateful for my nausea because I could hop up and wander away each time I wanted to escape the dialogue.

Finally, my "assigned" time passed, and he agreed to take me home. I was relieved to find my brother waiting for me.

Recently, I shared that story at a Relief Society activity when they asked for worst-date stories. Afterward, several ladies approached me and asked for more details. One friend said, "Boy, your mom's prayer sure saved you!" I had always known that getting sick at the restaurant was an act of divine providence, but it had never occurred to me that the credit belonged to my mother. I remembered President Packer's words again about the power of mother's prayers, and I understood.

It's true that because I am a mother with children of my own, my personal prayers have a new kind of urgency for two reasons: (1) Now I am responsible for needs beyond my own, and (2) I need a lot of help with this mom business. I spent plenty of time praying for more sleep or an end to colic or just enough time to take a shower, but I learned how desperate a mother's prayer can be when my son had a seizure and stopped breathing.

My husband held our son's blue body and tried to do artificial respiration while I frantically called 911 and pleaded for help. I prayed they would come quickly. I prayed they would know how to fix the problem. I prayed our son would be fine in the ambulance. I prayed through the noise of monitors and bustling doctors and nurses. I prayed as he was transferred to another hospital. I prayed as he underwent a battery of tests, and I prayed as I heard the results. My bishop and friend arrived at the hospital and gave me a blessing, and I prayed that their promises would come true. I prayed through medications and questions and sleepless nights. I prayed messages of gratitude when we were able to bring our son home, and I prayed relief as he slowly became his healthy, mischievous, two-year-old self. It was an early reminder that I absolutely could not mother without the teamwork of my Heavenly Father.

As my children grew and became vocal, Heavenly Father used them to teach me a lot of important lessons about faith and prayer. I recently viewed a Mormon Messages video that said, "Life doesn't come with a manual. It comes with a mother." I thought to myself, "Motherhood doesn't come with a manual either. It comes with children." Their needs and little personalities and even examples teach us a lot about how to be good mothers and, by extension, how to be good disciples of Jesus Christ.

By the time my son Grant was in kindergarten, he had prayed fish back to life, rain to stop, and the recovery of his lost brother at the mall. I'm positive the the sole reason my parents were not robbed on their mission in South Africa is that Grant and Clark prayed *every* day, "Please don't let the bad man steal Grandma and Grandpa's stuff." If our family is driving down the road in a snowstorm and cars are sliding off the road all around us, we know we should ask Grant to pray. He usually thinks of it first though.

Unfortunately, he's also sincere. Occasionally, there are the prayers that say, "Please bless the dinner that it won't be gross," or "Bless Natalie that she won't play with my toys."

A few years ago I had a blogging crisis of monumental proportions. Somehow, a year's worth of memory keeping was decimated in an instant, and no shred of digital evidence could be traced. I spent the majority of the next two days either at the computer or thinking about the computer. My children were not the recipients of much-deserved attention from me, and the attention they did get was mostly grumpy and distracted. I was frustrated.

I claimed the kids were more naughty than usual, but it doesn't take a rocket scientist to figure out what the *real* problem was. Nevertheless, this was Grant's dinner prayer one of those nights: "Thank you for this wonderful day. Sorry Clark and me made some sins. Please help us. And please bless the food. Amen."

I reflected on my own behavior, and when I put them all to bed that night, I apologized. I explained to them that my blog broke and got erased and that's why I was so grumpy and spent way too much time at the computer. Rather than begrudge my obvious failings, they were earnestly concerned about my blog and began asking many questions about how it "got disappeared." Grant had many theories. This one was my favorite: "I know. I know what happened. Maybe your blog was just tired, and it got so tired that it just went to sleep, and while it was asleep the computer just started re'rasing it." Then he offered to say a prayer about it and told me, "You and Daddy should probably say a prayer about that blog too."

If I were really a smart woman, I would have consulted Grant before we even began the backing-up-data process. I need to learn to put as much faith in my own prayers as I do in Grant's. My children are my prayer mentors. And I'm learning that since I am simply babysitting their little souls for God, He wants me to talk to Him about them more often. I don't usually make *huge* mistakes as a mother, but my days are riddled with missteps and flawed parenting, and these habits have made me pray more often than I ever did before. I need Heavenly Father more often. I need His help, His forgiveness, His strength, and often His compassion.

My children have taught me when to pray and what to pray about, but they've also taught me *how* to pray. My son Clark hates bad dreams and often prays to avoid them. One night several years ago, I overheard this prayer: "Dear Heavenly Father, please bless me that I won't have any bad dreams. But if I do, I won't be mad. But please bless me that I won't have bad dreams. Please help us that our days will be great. In the name of Jesus Christ, amen." There's much to learn in that prayer. He taught me that we can ask for what we want but that we also need to be willing to accept what comes. And we shouldn't be bitter. This is a lesson I've needed many, many times. From impatience with potty training to waiting on a job offer or a family move, learning to understand and accept the Lord's will has been essential to my contentment as a mother.

I sometimes joke that my prayers have saved my children's lives on many occasions—especially when I've prayed for strength to not kill them. Those years in the trenches of young motherhood are exhausting. A prayer before entering the battle of daily routines can be most helpful. One morning, I put my morning prayer in writing to capture the essence of that stage in life and to remember my dependence on my Heavenly Father.

Dear Heavenly Father,

I'm not sure I have the energy for today, so I'm asking for Your help. Please bless Natalie to take her medicine without screaming, gagging, and throwing up so she can get better. I need courage to start the job of helping my children pick up the playroom. Again. Help Matt to be ready for his finals and get done all the papers and work he needs to do so he can graduate in January. I need my husband back in the evenings so I don't harm my children when I put them to bed by myself every night. How do You do it, Heavenly Father? How do You not lose Your temper when no one listens to You? Help me be more like You.

Every time I think about all the laundry I need to do, I want to run away. I know it's a silly thing, but please give me the discipline I need to actually start it. I'm thankful I have a washing machine. I remember washing all my clothes by hand in Argentina, and I know I'm blessed, but I still need help to tackle the job ahead of me. Help me remember that my children are not adults, and they are not like me. They don't care if the house looks as clean today as it did yesterday. Help me be patient and understanding but still teach them responsibility.

I'm running out of Thanksgiving leftovers, so I should probably start cooking again. Help me to plan and be resourceful so I don't get overwhelmed at dinner time when the kids are all crazy and I have no ideas. I'm thankful we have food. And a warm house. Seriously, Heavenly Father, I'm so glad I have a place to stay warm and comfortable when the weather is so cold. Please bless those who aren't as lucky; help them find the shelter and care they need.

Finally, Heavenly Father, help me relax and face today with a good attitude. Forgive me for my mistakes and childish pouting. Help me be worthy of the blessings of my covenants because I need them. Help me remember how much I love my children and how much You do too. Bless me with the patience and kindness and charity I need to give them a good example and teach them all they need to know. Help me turn to You again when I start to forget. I'm sure we'll talk again really soon. I love You.

As I reread that prayer now, several years later, I feel a little silly, but mostly, I feel grateful. I can see that He heard me. I can see that He answered me. I survived those years, and so did my children. They are older now, but they continue to stretch me. Knowing that God answered those early prayers gives me confidence. He will continue to hear my prayers. Little by little, both my children and I will become the people He means for us to be.

My testimony of prayer has been multigenerational. My mother's prayers have been a source of strength for me through every decade of my life. My children's faith and sincere prayers have shown me how to have more confidence in prayer and more trust in the answers that come. And my own motherhood experience has helped me rely more on my Heavenly Father and the strength of the Atonement. Covenant mothers' hearts and minds constantly rely on divine help to accomplish the task of bringing children to Him. And since it is really His work too, it makes sense that He uses his living prophets to remind us He will help. He gives our prayers power. He gives *us* power. I'm so thankful for that help because I need it every day.

---

1 Boyd K. Packer, "These Things I Know," *Ensign*, May 2013.
2 Jeffrey R. Holland, "A Prayer for the Children," *Ensign*, May 2003.

OTHER BOOKS
BY STEPHANIE DIBB SORENSEN

Covenant Motherhood

My Neighbor
Susan Easton Black

LIKE MOST LATTER-DAY SAINT mothers of young sons, I was often on my knees asking the Lord to bless and protect my sons and help them learn lessons that would benefit their lives. Then, almost in a scripted motion, I would arise from my knees and move through the tasks of the day with little thought that an answer was forthcoming. It was not that I didn't think the Lord would protect my sons or teach them valuable lessons; it was just that I had much to do to meet the expectations of each day.

Mondays were particularly difficult. Not only did I have the usual daily tasks to do, but I also had the added expectation of a lesson and refreshments for family home evening.

Hoping the lesson "As I Have Loved You, Love One Another" would prove meaningful to my sons, I asked them, "Who would you like to serve in our neighborhood?"

"Let's do something nice for Sister Washburn," my youngest son, John, said.

Wasel Washburn was the elderly widow who lived next door. She had raised ten children, was a grandmother to eighty-seven grandchildren, and had untold multitudes of great-grandchildren.

My first thought was, *Why Sister Washburn? She already has attentive family members nearby who serve her.*

However, feeling duty bound to remember my next-door neighbor, I said to John, "We *should* do something nice for Sister Washburn." I then asked my other sons, "Would you like to serve Sister Washburn too?"

"I would like to pick flowers from her yard," my oldest son, Brian, said. He wanted to pick a large bouquet of flowers from her window box and give them to her.

My middle son, Todd, caught the drift of Brian's plan and added, "I would like to shovel her walks when it snows." His offer to shovel walks in mid-August caused both Todd and Brian to burst out laughing.

Not old enough to catch on to the family's middling ideas of service, John said, "I would like to bake cookies for Sister Washburn."

We baked cookies and picked flowers, but Sister Washburn remained more of an associate than a neighbor. She was the person the family awkwardly waved to if she happened to be outside as we hurried past.

But that changed a few months later.

The change began early one morning in November when I looked out the window and saw snow covering the ground. I awoke Todd, saying, "It snowed last night."

He couldn't believe my news or his misfortune. "I haven't waxed my skis," he said. "How could it have snowed already?"

I told Todd not to think about waxing skis, building a snowman, or even throwing snowballs. "Today is your first chance to shovel Sister Washburn's walks!" I said.

"Oh, you remembered," he moaned.

Yes, I remembered his joy as he'd imagined shoveling her walks in August. He grudgingly looked for a coat, a hat, and gloves and reluctantly meandered out the back door, only to return in a few moments.

"I cannot possibly shovel her walks," he said.

After assuring my growing son that he certainly could shovel her walks, to my amazement, Todd said, "I can't shovel her walks. Sister Washburn has already done them."

I was astonished at his words and felt a twinge of embarrassment, wondering if someone had seen the elderly woman shoveling her walks when they knew our family lived next door.

"I am embarrassed!" I said to Todd. "Our whole family should have shoveled her walks."

Todd smiled big "You think you are embarrassed now—wait till you look out the window."

As I gazed out the window, I saw Sister Washburn shoveling *our* walks. If that had been the only act of charity Wasel Washburn extended to our family, perhaps she would have remained just the elderly woman next door. But there were more acts of kindness to follow.

One such act occurred on what started out as a typical Wednesday. With rote routine, I still prayed that the Lord would bless and protect my children and help them learn valuable lessons in life. That morning, my sons left home and walked to the Rock Canyon Elementary School, and I walked in the opposite direction to Brigham Young University.

The day went as planned for Brian, John, and me, but not for Todd. While playing on the school playground, he became dizzy. He told his teacher, and she sent him to the principal's office with a note requesting that I come to take him home. The principal or his office staff must have had a huge agenda that morning because no one called me. Todd waited in the office, hoping he would be noticed and I would be called. But as time passed, he grew impatient and determined to take the matter into his own hands.

Todd left the principal's office and ran home, only to discover the doors were locked. He tried to get into the house through a window near the front door but had no luck. He tried other windows with the same result. Feeling sick and frustrated, he walked to the side yard, sat down, and began to cry. As he was wiping his tears, he heard the voice of our neighbor Sister Washburn. She was standing in her side yard as if waiting for him. She comforted Todd and took him into her home. She had him lie down on her couch while she fixed him lunch and made homemade rolls. When I arrived home, Todd was happy, and Sister Washburn was happy too.

Her account of the incident differs slightly from Todd's. She told me she served as a patron in the Provo Utah Temple every Wednesday. On that day, she had been at the temple all morning and was planning to stay there through the early afternoon, but she received a strong impression that she was needed at home. Rather than ignore the impression, she left the temple and returned to her house. She then telephoned her ten children, hoping to find which child needed immediate help. After learning that all was well with them and their families, she concluded that something must be wrong next door. She walked out of her house toward her side yard and found my distraught son Todd.

This episode says as much about me as it does my neighbor. Sister Washburn felt needed at home. I had no such feeling. I was confident that my children were enjoying a wonderful day at school.

What would anyone give for a neighbor like Sister Washburn? What could I learn from her that was missing in my life? Through the ensuing seventeen years, Sister Washburn became my dearest friend, confidant, and adopted grandmother to my sons. She was no longer the neighbor who happened to live next door—she was an intricate part of our lives. My sons mowed her lawn, told her about their days at school, and shared their accomplishments. They picked flowers from our yard to give her and cheerfully shoveled her walks without being asked. She came over to our house often and became as much a part of our lives as any family member could.

At age ninety-six, Wasel Washburn became very ill. Her children, grandchildren, and great-grandchildren rushed to her bedside. I was invited to see her for a few moments.

As she lay in bed looking feebler than I had seen her before, she asked, "How are my boys?"

I knew she wasn't asking about her sons; she was asking about my sons. I was grateful to say, "They love you dearly and will cherish your memory always."

In August 1993, I bade farewell to Sister Washburn but will never forget the important lessons she taught me about prayer and inspiration as I guide my family through life's many experiences.

OTHER BOOKS AND AUDIO BOOKS
BY SUSAN EASTON BLACK

400 Questions and Answers series

100 Women of Character

100 Men of Character

Philosophies and Pioneer Pianos
Josi S. Kilpack

MANY YEARS AGO, A HIGH councilor with a houseful of teenagers gave a talk in sacrament meeting about parenting and said, "Before I had children, I had all kinds of philosophies about how to raise them. Now I have children and no philosophies."

He went on to talk about how raising children was the ultimate lesson in humility and that most days it was a swing-by-the-seat-of-your-pants experience he could never have truly prepared for. It was a beautiful talk . . . for the kind of parents who needed it.

I was a new mother, and my philosophies about parenting were still bright and shiny. I believed that by doing things a certain way, I could guarantee an outcome. For instance, children who took music lessons never questioned their testimonies. Having a happy marriage would ensure my children always had good dating and marriage relationships. And going to church every Sunday would stave off most of the problems teenagers in non-church-attending families encountered. There were hundreds of smaller philosophies, but they were similar in design. Like a math equation, the right parenting choices equaled perfect children. This analogy alone should have given me pause; I've never been good at math.

Fast-forward about ten years. I am a not-so-young mother of four now, and my oldest child is thirteen. Like the pianos left behind by pioneers when they realized the toll it took to carry nonessentials, I had left many of my early philosophies about parenting along the wayside. I didn't care if my daughters' shoes matched their clothes. We didn't eat dinner together every night, and my children's rooms were disaster areas. Many things from my earlier list of "I would never let my kid do that!" had been done. I felt I'd learned to focus on the *important* philosophies—music lessons, chores, athletics, homework, Church, scripture study on those nights when all the kids were tired enough to sit still. My kids were doing great—proof of my good parenting. *I* was validated in their nearly perfect lives and took great pride in the results of my efforts.

And then around midnight on a Tuesday in March, there was a knock on our bedroom door. Groggy and annoyed, I told whatever child had awakened us to come in. Instead of one of the younger kids reporting a nightmare or telling me they felt sick, it was my thirteen-year-old. She asked me to come out, so I grabbed my robe and met her in the hallway.

She'd been crying, hard. I asked what was wrong, and she told me she'd felt dark and hopeless for weeks and had been lying in her bed for hours that night thinking about suicide and growing increasingly convinced that it was the only thing that would make her feel better.

The words hit me like boulders, and my brain scrambled to figure out how I was supposed to respond to this. Had there ever been a Relief Society lesson on what the protocol was for dealing with a suicidal child? This was not what nearly perfect parents were supposed to face. This was not how a nearly perfect child was supposed to feel.

Her father gave her a blessing. I offered to sleep in her room, but she didn't want that. Instead, I lay in my bed the rest of the night staring at the ceiling and feeling what I *thought* was the last of my parenting philosophies slip through my fingers. Was this what that high councilor had meant? That he had no philosophies because he'd learned they guaranteed nothing? *That* was suddenly something I could relate to. I had lost a brother to suicide, and my husband had lost a sister to the self-medication of her mental illness. In light of those losses, our daughter's thoughts were terrifying to us. We knew where they could take her—where they could take all of us.

My parenting philosophies had not included my children needing therapy or medications, but within weeks, our daughter was immersed in both as we tried to find her a way out of her struggles. The way out was a complicated path, and for the next three years, she continued to battle depression, medication increases, suicidal thoughts, feelings of self-hatred, and impulses to cut herself when the pain was too much.

She didn't like feeling as though she was disappointing her dad and me, so she became an expert at putting on a good face, a face her father and I wanted to believe so much that we usually did. We did everything we could think of to help her, and we prayed constantly. More than anything, I wanted Heavenly Father to take it away. Take the struggle away from her. Take it away from us. We were *good* people; she was a *good* girl.

But I could not get over the fact that all of my philosophies on parenting seemed to have been proven false. My confidence was shaken, my expectations that had once been so clear were now vague and limited, and I struggled with feelings of self-doubt and embarrassment. Without those philosophies of parenting—those guarantees I'd taken such comfort in—I felt adrift and unsure of myself and my role. I couldn't help but feel that if I'd been a better mother, my daughter wouldn't be having these problems.

When she was sixteen and a half, things took a bad turn. She had dated a boy who turned out to be someone none of us should have trusted. We'd forbidden the relationship. She'd reacted by taking the relationship underground. We'd sniffed it out and brought down the hammer. I didn't know how to talk to her, and she was so angry and hurt that she had no interest in talking to me anyway; instead, she pulled further inside herself.

I felt like a deer in the headlights, incapable of knowing which direction to go, unsure of my course, and certain that any second now something could happen that none of us would ever recover from.

I was waiting to pick her up from karate one evening and watched her come out the front doors with a classmate. In my mind, I asked what was going to happen to her? I had asked the question many times. Would she ever forgive us for forcing her to give up the relationship she wanted so much? Would the depression get worse? Would the self-harm become more violent? Would she continue to hurt this much forever? Would she turn to self-medicating as so many people did when they couldn't find wellness?

I had become used to not getting answers to these questions—maybe I didn't really want the answers in the first place—but as she reached the steps of the building, she turned to her friend and laughed, something I saw very little of these days. In an instant, she transformed before my eyes. The braces on her teeth disappeared, the acne we'd battled along with her depression cleared, her hair became darker, thicker, and better tended. In that instant, she was not my sixteen-year-old daughter. She was a young woman with a history and future that were not mine to carry for her. I realized in that moment, in a way I'd never known before, that *her* struggles were part of *her* journey. Through them, she was learning things she needed to know. I could not take her struggles from her. I was never supposed to.

Amid the hope of this moment was another slap of hopelessness. If it wasn't up to me to make her better, what *was* my role? Was I to sit back and simply watch? Another instant insight struck me, and I realized that while I couldn't make these things go away, I had to *stop* feeling so dang sorry for myself. I had to stop worrying about the way her struggles reflected on *me*. *I* had to stop feeling so hopeless. Those were choices within my power that I hadn't looked at because I so wanted to fix *her*.

The vision and the thoughts that followed lasted only a moment. By the time she reached the car, she was my brace-faced teenage daughter again. Circumstances didn't change because of the vision I'd had. She still battled depression. Our relationship continued to struggle. Her dad and I still wondered what to do for her. We continued to pray, but the prayers changed a little bit. Rather than just praying for her to get better—though we still asked for that—we asked for God to walk this road with her and us. I tried to process her experiences through the lens of "What can *I* learn from this?" instead of "What is *she* learning?" When the fear crept in, as it often did, I evaluated whether or not I was doing my part as well as I could—did she know I loved her? When had I last told her so? Was I making the tools she needed available?

While I don't know that my change in perspective made a difference for her, I felt more peace and hope for her future, which was a great blessing for me. In time, she gained insight and understanding into herself and began to find healing. I gained insight and understanding too and came to realize that most of those philosophies I'd held on to for so long were more like superstitions. It made me feel better to have them and to believe that 1 + 1 = 2, but people were not equations. There was little correlation between my children meeting an expectation of mine and, therefore, avoiding hardship. The things that mattered were all about my relationship with my Father in Heaven and their relationship with Him. When I was in a good place spiritually, I was a better mother to my daughter, and that was really the only thing I had control over. It was rather shocking to realize just how much I had to learn and how much my daughter had taught me.

Her last year of high school was a far more positive experience than the others had been. She got into the only college she had ever wanted to attend and graduated from high school with honors. She left home just two weeks after graduation due to a summer program she'd been accepted into and has loved her college experience. She comes home when she can, and I am always so excited to see her and hear about her life. Sometimes I marvel at the distance she has crossed since those dark years. I could not be more proud of the good choices she's made. I could not be more grateful that she is doing so well.

But I miss her. And I worry about her. I know she will have more trials—just like I have, just like everyone has. In the years since her struggles drove my husband and me to our knees, we have been blindsided by other situations with our children that we didn't see coming either. I've felt similar hopelessness—the fear for their futures has threatened to consume me at times—but I haven't forgotten what I learned through those early experiences of parenting a teenager. Perhaps the most important thing I have learned is to be more loving and less judgmental, to try to see my children as individuals instead of test subjects, and to encourage the search for answers to their specific problems through prayer.

These days, I reflect on that high councilor's talk very differently than I did when I first heard it. Having a plan for raising children is a good idea, and the positive skills and habits I have helped teach them will bless their lives. But nothing I do can change the fact that my children have things to learn that I can't teach them. When I truly understand that, I realize I don't want to take their trials away because without trials, there is no growth.

I don't remember how that high councilor ended his talk all those years ago, but I think I can guess for myself. I think he went on to tell us that the best resource for parenting is our Father in Heaven, that love is always the answer, and that faith and consistency and patience and humility are all virtues earned through the refining fires of the toughest callings we'll ever have. I think that high counselor wished us young parents luck, reminded us to pray, and told us to help our children form a bond with God that would help them through their trials more than we ever could.

I'm not done raising my children, and I still have much to learn, but I know better how to lead my children, guide them, and walk beside them than I could ever have imagined when I started this journey. I can only hope they learn as much from me as I've learned from them.

OTHER BOOKS AND AUDIO BOOKS
BY JOSI S. KILPACK

Daisy

Shannon's Hope

Sadie Hoffmiller series

The Healing Power of Prayer
Jeri Gilchrist

I WAS FIGHTING A LOSING BATTLE . . .

My son was anxiously awaiting his mission call. This created quite an air of excitement in our home. Like many families, we had a contest going to see who would come the closest to picking Tyler's destination. The world map was filling up, and the anticipation level was at an all-time high as the call was expected to come any day.

When his call finally came, the contest actually came down to figuring out miles between two players, but as a mother, I was already a winner. My heart swelled with pride because I had a son, a missionary who had been called to serve in the Finland Helsinki Mission.

The days seemed to fly, and soon we found ourselves heading to the MTC. When we got there, we watched the movie and listened to the speaker. I couldn't guess who held on to him longer when saying good-bye, myself or his youngest brother, Bryan, but I do recall going home and sitting at the computer for what seemed years, hoping for that first e-mail that he was all settled in.

Over the next couple of months, we loved to receive letters that told of Tyler's experiences. On the very day he entered the MTC, they started learning to pray in Finish. My heart was full, and my tears were constant, but they were always tears of joy.

How I prayed for my son. I prayed for his safety. I prayed for his understanding of a new language. I prayed for his love for a new land and new way of life, and most of all, I prayed for his testimony to increase so he could feel the love of his Savior and a greater desire to teach the gospel. There was a constant prayer within my heart. Surely these were the prayers of every missionary's mother.

Our family loved sending creative same-day-delivery packages. We sent anything from Krispy Kreme doughnuts to pizza parties. We got some strange requests from fellow roomies. We felt connected with those missionaries as we tried to fill their requests.

Very quickly, the letters and e-mails changed as we saw our son growing and changing in ways that were wonderful for a mother to hear. He was having experiences and learning the gospel at a deeper level than he had before. In those quiet moments when his letters came, telling of the incredible experiences he had already begun to have, I was so grateful for the peace in my heart for where my son was and for what he was doing. He was becoming the type of man our Heavenly Father wanted him to be.

Time came for the Finland missionaries to leave. We could no longer meet the missionaries at the airport, and though I understood this rule and the reasons for it, I wondered at the two years I would not get to see him. That was a long time to go without seeing a missionary. I decided it was important to obey the rule . . . but could I just bend it a titch? (The answer here should be *no*!) I knew we should not "meet" the missionaries, but if only I could "see" my missionary, I could let him go for two years.

My husband and youngest son were out in the parking lot of the airport driving around and around through the passenger drop-off area while I was up in the "look out" area, where passengers enter to check in luggage.

Suddenly, my cell phone rang, and I jumped as if I had been caught. (Yes, my conscience was working hard on me).

"The blue goose has entered the coop," my husband's voice spoke in a quiet undertone (he was always one to help with an undercover op). "It's on you. We will rendezvous at the drop-off location for a debriefing." (Obviously, he was enjoying the "undercover op" a bit too much.) "I'm going in for a closer observation," he said, and then the line dropped.

This was my cue. The blue bus (code name: Blue Goose) that brought the missionaries from the MTC had entered the airport and was unloading.

I jumped behind a palm frond tree that stood in the corner of the overhead area and watched and waited, and then I saw my missionary. He walked in with the group of other missionaries. He looked so handsome and so happy. That was all I needed. That vision could carry me for two years. I turned to leave, reassured that all was well, when I was stopped dead in my tracks.

There stood a beautiful Polynesian woman behind me with raised eyebrows. "Are you looking for someone?" she asked. Aw sheesh; I was busted. All I wanted was a glimpse of my son, to know he was fine and I could handle what was ahead of me. Now I felt like I was caught being disobedient.

"No, I found who I was looking for."

I mustered up a weak smile and took a step forward when she asked, "Which missionary is yours?"

How did she know? I wondered.

"That one," I said, proudly pointing to my missionary. I told her his name and where he was going, then told her I needed to make my get away before I was caught.

She smiled at me and said, "Your missionary will do great things."

I thanked her and ran back to my husband a little puffed up with pride but so thankful to see my son so happy. Yes, back to my not-so-happy husband, who, by this time, had circled the airport countless times while doing our covert operation.

When Ty called us on the cell phone from the airport, the first thing he asked was, "Mom, were you here?"

Yikes! The lady had told on me. It didn't pay to be disobedient, even if it was just a titch.

Once Tyler got to Helsinki, his love for the people and the country grew, and he gained greater knowledge of the gospel, and more importantly, his testimony was strengthened, just as he had been promised in his patriarchal blessing.

While with his second companion in Helsinki, Tyler became very ill. He had previously had problems with migraines, but now they had worsened to the point that they were coming in clusters. Finland had limited options for Tyler, so the mission's area doctor contacted us from Frankfurt, Germany, and instructed us to contact Ty's doctor here to send different medications to see if anything would work. It was a frustrating effort for everyone involved.

I had always prayed for my missionary. We as parents prayed for him individually; we prayed for him as a family. We prayed for him as a ward. The mission began to pray for my son. Yet, soon he was so sick he was no longer able to go out tracting.

I remember an e-mail my son sent home that spoke of his feeling so awful he couldn't do the work he was sent there to do. But he had a very loyal and patient companion. They would try to bake cookies and take them to neighbors or the less-active members, and when that became too much, the two of them would sit by the window and try to reach out to the people walking on the sidewalk below. If they could make any sort of contact, they'd toss copies of the Book of Mormon down to them. As I read Ty's e-mail that night, a tear rolled down my face.

I knelt in prayer—again—but my prayers had changed from those days of fun MTC packages and hiding behind plants.

Late one night, Tyler's mission president's voice came over the phone. My missionary was in his office. He explained that it was in Ty's best interest to receive medical treatment back in the States. If they were able to help him, he could come back, but while receiving treatment, Ty would be released as a missionary for the Church. He would be leaving in the morning.

The president put my son on the phone, and his voice shook with emotion. He was never one to show a lot of emotion, so just hearing his voice was almost more than I could take.

"I failed," he said. "I didn't do what I was sent here to do. I don't want to come home." Then he cried.

Silently, I prayed for the right thing to say. "How can you say you failed, son? You have no idea what lives you have touched—so far. You come home, and we'll get you feeling good again. We'll do all we can to get you back out there, okay?"

"I love you, Mom."

"I love you too. Everything is going to be okay, I promise."

The call ended, and my heart ached for my son. I had promised him that everything would be okay, but how could I possibly know that?

Two days later, I stood waiting anxiously to see Ty. When he walked through the gate, I was choked with tears. It was good to see him again, but he looked terrible.

His suit was loose; his face was pale and withdrawn. The pressure in the cabin of the plane had done nothing to help his migraine, and after a twenty-hour flight, he just wanted to go home and go to bed. All the way there, he kept saying, "I want to go back." He had tears in his eyes, and my heart was so heavy I felt I couldn't bear it.

The mission department had a specialist they'd referred us to, and I had set up an appointment for Tyler for the following day. They took x-rays, drew his blood, and tried several medications.

During those months, from the time Tyler left for his mission on through his treatment, I saw a change in my son. He grew from a child to a man. He relied on his Savior and gained a greater knowledge and testimony than I had witnessed in him before. He never questioned why, though I know he was hurt and disappointed in the outcome. Still, he persisted and served in any capacity he could during the time of his treatment and while awaiting word that he could return to the mission field. I was grateful in those days that Tyler's test of strength was one endured with faith and love for his Savior.

However, at the time of this experience, I often found *myself* wondering why. Here was my son, willing, wanting, and worthy to serve. He had loved his time as a missionary. Why did it have to be cut short? Our Father in Heaven could have healed Ty. Why didn't He?

I watched my son, who was ill with the migraines and the side effects from medications.

There were those who didn't know or fully understand what was happening who made insensitive comments that only added to the hurt and disappointment already being felt.

Negative thoughts crept into my mind, and soon the hurt festered, and I felt frustration at the unfairness of it all. Tyler didn't deserve this.

It took five months to break the cycle of cluster migraines he was having, and therefore, the advice was given that he not return to the mission field. I will never forget the look on my son's face when he received the news. The sorrow and dejection was beyond my ability to express. Still, Tyler never muttered an angry word.

No one is exempt from trial, pain, or adversity in this life. There is no way around it. We all have to go through it. It was in that moment, I realized just how much Tyler had really grown. He was given an honorable release.

I began to realize that I had "the protective mother bear syndrome," which, I would suppose, was natural. Mothers protect their young, sometimes to a fault, but my thoughts were turning to self-pity that could have been destructive, and if I did not stop, it would consume me.

In those months, I had begun to feel helpless, that praying was almost a hopeless cause. I couldn't demand or force the desires of my heart to happen, no matter how righteous I thought they were. I felt I was fighting a losing battle.

How wrong I was.

I am grateful to know that no matter how deeply I love my children, my Heavenly Father loves them even more. I needed a blessing for myself, and how grateful I am for that blessing. My prayers started to change as I asked for a change of heart and a way to know what was best to help my son. Slowly, my whole outlook changed, and my heart was lifted. I felt assured that it really was going to be all right, as I had told Ty it would be. It wasn't an empty promise; I truly felt it.

But even with that assurance, I continued to battle bouts of negative thoughts. But I knew that if I was receiving reassurance, Heavenly Father had not deserted my son or myself. I became stronger because of this experience.

My son was developing character, strength, and testimony, all that I had hoped he would gain on a mission. He had not been robbed of the blessings of serving, but rather, he still had the opportunity to serve in other capacities.

Through the prayers of a mother for her son, I finally began to put things into perspective. I put them into an eternal perspective. I realized again and again the tender mercy and love our Father in Heaven had for each of us.

I may never know why the answer to our prayers to Tyler's healing was no at the time, but I do know that not all prayers are answered immediately. As I look back on that experience several years later, I see how many blessings have come because of that event in our lives.

Tyler came home, and because the timing was right, he met and married his beautiful wife, Felicia, in the temple. They have given me two adorable grandkids, Ryker and Mykenzie. Ty's career is such that he comes in contact every day with many people who know nothing of the gospel, so he has opportunities to let them know of his beliefs through his actions and example. He was also able to give one of his missionary companions a job when he came home and continues to have contact with some of his companions to this day.

I know I learned more about the mercy and love our Savior has for each of us. Because of my experience, I will never question the power or purpose of prayer, and I will be forever grateful for the priesthood. I realize I have a Father in Heaven who has infinitely more wisdom than I and always has our best interest at heart; we just need to trust in His will. Perhaps Tyler was sent to Helsinki so I could better learn these things and so he could more fully convert me.

OTHER BOOKS AND AUDIO BOOKS
BY JERI GILCHRIST

Shadow of the Crown

The Perfect Plan

Out of Nowhere

Our Partnership with God
Toni Sorenson

Yes, God does answer prayers. I'm convinced there is a priority line in heaven for the prayers that slip from the tongues of anxious mothers. I believe there is a never-ending line of angels ready to be dispatched to aid the mothers whose prayers ascend in faith and love and often in desperation for their children.

One summer afternoon, I found myself pacing back and forth in front of our house. My heart was breaking, and I didn't know what to do. My oldest son had been injured, and two doctors told me he would lose his vision in one eye. They said there was nothing more they could do. My heart told me otherwise, and I silently begged Heavenly Father to hear my prayer, to find a way to heal my son—*our* son.

Shortly after that, while I was still pacing the sidewalk, a car pulled into our driveway. It was a friend I had not seen in months.

"I don't know why I'm here," she said almost apologetically, "but I was driving down the road, and a little voice whispered for me to turn around and come see you."

An angel had been dispatched to answer my prayer. My friend just happened to be a nurse, a nurse who happened to know an eye surgeon, who happened to know the latest treatment to prevent my son from losing his vision.

Coincidence?

I vote with the British statesman Sir William Temple on that issue. He said, "When I pray, coincidences happen, and when I don't, they don't."

As a single mother of six children, it's been a challenge to meet their needs, a role I've not always fulfilled to my complete satisfaction and,

I'm certain, not to theirs. There have been times when I've fallen to my knees, exhausted in every way. There have been times when I have been out of energy, money, patience, and even hope. In those times, prayer was what restored my resources.

At a time when I could not afford to buy a bicycle for my five-year-old son, a shiny red bike appeared on our front porch one snowy Christmas morning. When another son tried out for the basketball team, I silently prayed that he would *not* make it because I could not afford to pay for the expensive shoes required. But he made the team, and it just so happened that a mother of one of his teammates bought a pair of shoes that would not fit her son and could not be returned. She gave them to my son because they were a perfect fit for him.

Some coincidence.

Most recently, when my funds were ripped away to pay unexpected medical bills, I found myself in need of a suit for my soon-departing missionary son. Again, the answer to that prayer came in the form of a dear friend who did not understand the compulsion to buy my son a suit but said, "Please, let us do this."

"Twist my arm," I joked, knowing exactly why that prompting had come.

Most of the prayers I pray are not for material blessings for my children but for spiritual strength, moral integrity, or a turn of their hearts to their Savior. When I was a child, the only time my mother ever taught me to pray was when we heard the siren of an ambulance. "Father," she would say as we drove along, "please bless the people who are in need of that help, and we thank Thee that it's not us."

Now, when my children are not with me and I hear a siren, a silent prayer very similar to the one my mother uttered goes forth from my heart. Usually, one of my children will get a phone call from me that goes something like this:

"I just heard a siren. Are you all right?"

"I'm fine. The siren you heard was in Utah, Mom; I'm in Florida. No matter how loud it was, it wasn't for me."

Sometimes we mothers pray for our children and don't even understand why. I know a mother who was making dinner one night when the Spirit told her to "get down on your knees and pray for your son!"

She dropped the spatula and fell to her knees. "Father, I don't know what kind of trouble Daryl is in, but You do. Please bless him and keep him safe."

She looked at the clock on the stove and noted the time. When she called her son who lived in Hawaii, he sounded just fine.

"This afternoon I fell to my knees and prayed for you," she told Daryl. "I didn't even know what to pray for; I just prayed."

He was silent for a long time, and then she heard him sniffle. "What time was that, Mother?"

She told him.

He gasped. "At that very hour, I was driving home along the narrow, winding road above the cliffs; I fell asleep at the wheel. I swear to you, hands shook my shoulders and woke me just in time to keep me from plunging through the guardrail."

છ

My heart breaks for the mothers whose children have died despite their prayers. Or, like me, they blame themselves because they didn't do enough to keep their child from letting go of the iron rod, even momentarily. If you carry an unbearable burden of sorrow or guilt, I beg you to forgive—forgive yourself. For you, Christ atoned. No one understands better the anguish and heartache of knowing that a beloved child is wandering in the mists of darkness, lost and vulnerable. Christ's Atonement covers your sorrow, your guilt, and your fears, and it covers your child's choices.

The Atonement is so much more than we realize, and I ask that as you read these words, you take a deep breath. Clear your mind and heart. Let the Spirit of a perfect Parent whisper to you how much He loves you and trusts you and assures you that you are not alone and will never be alone in this mighty work called raising children unto Him.

In 3 Nephi 27:29, the Savior admonishes, "Ask, and ye shall receive." This doesn't mean you will receive exactly what you ask for—not even if you are a faithful, loving mother—but you will receive.

Elder Richard G. Scott explained that prayer "does not assure that you will get what you *want*. It does guarantee that, if worthy, you will get what you *need*, as judged by a Father that loves you perfectly, who wants your eternal happiness even more than do you."[1]

I've prayed many prayers for my children that appear to have gone unheard and certainly unanswered. So have all mothers. One friend, the mother of a teenage son battling depression and Satan's fiercest temptations, prayed and prayed for her son's safety. Then one night, she got the telephone call every mother fears most—that something terrible had happened to her child.

For a time, she held herself responsible. "If I had only prayed with greater faith. If I'd gone to the temple that day. If only I had . . ."

For a time, that mother seemed beyond consolation, but her reservoir of faith bore deeper into her spirit than she realized. The teaching of Joseph Smith seemed particularly relevant: "After your tribulations, if you . . . exercise fervent prayer and faith in the sight of God always, He shall give unto you knowledge by His Holy Spirit, yea by the unspeakable gift of the Holy Ghost, that has not been revealed since the world was until now."[2]

In her grief, *only* the Holy Ghost could truly comfort her, and when He did, she told me, "My prayers changed from, 'Keep my son safe' to 'Hold him, Father, in your arms until I can be there to hold him again.'"

That mother's faith was not forsaken. She lost her son in mortality but not in eternity. Does her sorrow leave? No. Not for a moment. But her suffering? That's been abated through the Atonement.

I have never liked the commercial holiday we call Mother's Day because it makes me feel inadequate at the most important work I'll ever do. For years, I hated the little red and white carnations passed out after church services. Then I learned about a Sunday School teacher in West Virginia whose namesake daughter petitioned the Church to honor her mother for her decades of service. She and the Church made an agreement, and because Anna's mother's favorite flower was the carnation, a worldwide tradition was born. Red flowers to the living mothers and white in memory of those mothers who had passed on. That makes me think of my own mother and grandmothers and great-grandmothers who are dead. Are they not the angels dispatched to serve my children and me? Who would be better suited to answer such family prayers?

Mothers, today as I write this, I pray for you and for myself. We must unite as women of God to do the most important work of all: to nurture and nourish the bodies and spirits of Father's most noble and strongest children. We must have faith in the faith He has placed in us. No more questioning if we are up to the great responsibility. He chose us to do this work. He will elevate us to the task if we will pray for His help. He will give us wisdom and inspiration beyond anything we could concoct on our own. We are partners with the God of all creation. Our Savior's work is to bring to pass the immortality and eternal life of these precious children. I assure you, He is very, very, very good at the work that He does.

Someone once admitted to me, "I don't know why I have been blessed with such obedient children." Another mother wept as she said, "I don't know why I have been given such disobedient spirits to mother."

Let's stop asking why and start figuring out how. Let's pray to see the children in our arms and in our homes as God the Father sees them. When I was beyond frustrated with one of my teenagers, I nearly lost my own vision because I could not see the potential in that child. All I could focus on were the problems. But then I listened to the inspired words of a patriarch telling us all what Father thought of that child.

The Lord's vision is perfect.

We can't see beyond the bend, but He can.

We might not have the answers to the hard questions, but He does.

❧

It was my privilege to spend Mother's Day in prison not so long ago. I was there to teach and testify of Jesus Christ, but like always, I was the one who learned. I learned from a woman named Ivy, who was serving a long-term sentence for drug trafficking.

"I'm here because of my mother," she said.

"Explain," I said.

"When I was fifteen, I got involved with a gang. Within weeks, I was selling drugs on the streets. Mama knew I was up to no good, and she said, 'I'll pray for you.' I didn't want her to, but Mama had been praying for me all my life, and I knew I couldn't stop her.

"When I was sixteen, she stepped up her praying. I'd come home and find her asleep on her knees at her bedside, her Bible clasped in her hands.

"It wasn't long before her prayers started to get answered. I got arrested. The cops started watching me. The harder she prayed, the harder the police came down on me. Finally, I robbed a store and ended up here. I thank God that I'm here with a chance to turn my life around, and I thank Mama for never ceasing to pray for me."

Ivy's story reminded me of Alma the Elder praying for his namesake son, who belonged to a gang and who wreaked havoc on the good and righteous. Imagine how the history of the Book of Mormon would be changed if Alma had not offered a parent's prayer. I can't help but believe that Alma's mother offered up a prayer or two herself.

❧

We can't do this thing called mothering on our own, but with His help, we can love the unlovable and have patience with the child whose behavior is like fingernails on the chalkboard of our limits. You know the joke that says if Isaac had been a teenager, it would not have been a sacrifice for Abraham.

Toddlers. Teenagers. Grown kids with kids of their own. No matter. Once we are mothers, we will always be mothers. We will never stop loving and carrying and being concerned. That's how Father feels about us. That's how our revered Heavenly Mother surely feels. Wonder, if you will, what prayers She has prayed on your behalf.

Please don't buy into Satan's lie that you're on your own, that you've failed. Yes, we can and should all do better, but our best is good enough, no matter what our kids tell us or what they do. Even our Heavenly Parents could and would not manipulate their children's agency. Consequently, one third were lost in the war in heaven, while others choose to turn away during the war that continues to rage on earth.

❧

Now, I ask one thing of you that you might not ask for yourself. Pray for you. Pray for your ability to enjoy your children, to see what God sees in them, pray for your mind to expand and your creativity in nurturing your children to increase. Pray for whatever skills and resources you need to parent the children who are your stewardship.

Take care of yourself so you can take better care of your children.

Equip yourself with knowledge and experience and challenges that make you a better person. Splurge on yourself once in a while so your children can see that you value yourself so they too will value themselves.

When I was investigating the Church many years ago, an Apostle was kind enough to oblige me with his time and wisdom. One of the things he told me was that Joseph Smith went to the grove to petition God because it was behind their family cabin, in that now-sacred grove of trees, that young Joseph had often seen his mother go to pray.

Let your children see you on your knees. Let them hear you pray for them. Let them hear you pray for forgiveness and let them see you receive it and move on with your day, determined to do better. Let them hear you pour your heart out in gratitude for every single blessing.

When you have doubts, please don't hesitate to express them in prayer. Be honest. Be open. Be willing.

We all make mistakes. Take heart in the words of the Prophet Joseph, who admitted, "I have called to mind all the past moments of my life, and am left to mourn and shed tears of sorrow for my folly in suffering the adversary of my soul to have so much power over me as he has had in times past. But God is merciful and has forgiven my sins, and I rejoice that he sendeth forth the Comforter unto as many as believe and humbleth themselves before him.[3]

Mothers, rejoice! Take a deep breath. Clear your minds and hearts. Let the Spirit of a perfect Parent whisper to you how much He loves you and trusts you and assures you that you are not alone and will never be alone in this mighty work called raising children unto Him.

1 Richard G. Scott, "Trust in the Lord," *Ensign*, Nov. 1995.

2 History of the Church 3:296.

3 Joseph Smith, *The Personal Writings of Joseph Smith*, 238; standardized.

OTHER BOOKS AND AUDIO BOOKS
BY TONI SORENSON

Redemption Road

Heroes of the Book of Mormon

Behold Your Little Ones

Mommy, Do I Have to Serve a Mission?

Master

Messiah

The Shaken Earth

Refined by Christ

Defined by Christ